ASTROLOGY

PISCES

BY ABBY DOTY

WWW.APEXEDITIONS.COM

Apex is distributed by North Star Editions:
sales@northstareditions.com | 888-417-0195

Produced for Apex by Red Line Editorial.

Photographs ©: Shutterstock Images, cover (illustration, constellation), cover (background), 1, 4–5, 9, 10–11, 12–13, 15, 16–17, 18–19, 20, 21, 24–25, 26–27, 29; iStockphoto, 6; Charles Walker Collection/Alamy, 7; Kevin Mazur/Getty Images Entertainment/Getty Images, 22–23

Library of Congress Control Number: 2025939153

ISBN
979-8-89250-787-5 (hardcover)
979-8-89250-816-2 (paperback)
979-8-89250-873-5 (ebook pdf)
979-8-89250-845-2 (hosted ebook)

Printed in the United States of America
Mankato, MN
012026

NOTE TO PARENTS AND EDUCATORS

Apex books are designed to build literacy skills in striving readers. Exciting, high-interest content attracts and holds readers' attention. The text is carefully leveled to allow students to achieve success quickly. Additional features, such as bolded glossary words for difficult terms, help build comprehension.

TABLE OF CONTENTS

CHAPTER 1

THE FISH

Pisces is a large **constellation**. Its shape looks like two fish linked by a rope. *Pisces* means “the fish” in Latin.

In northern parts of the world, Pisces is easiest to see in the fall.

Pisces is one of the earliest recorded constellations. People first wrote about it thousands of years ago. They told stories about it, too.

Pisces is one of 48 constellations that Ptolemy wrote about. He was a Greek thinker in the 100s CE.

When people in Egypt died, they were sometimes buried in coffins that had paintings based on constellations.

FAST FACT

Some Egyptian tombs and coffins have paintings of the Pisces fish.

One Roman story connects Pisces to the goddess Venus. She and her son faced a monster. They tied themselves together with a rope. Then they jumped into a river. They changed into fish to hide.

ANOTHER GODDESS

Another story links Pisces with a Syrian goddess. A giant egg fell from the sky into a river. Fish rolled it onto land. The goddess hatched from this egg.

The Syrian goddess Atargatis had ties to both Pisces and water. People built temples for her.

CHAPTER 2

SIGNS AND STARS

Pisces is one of the **zodiac** signs. Each sign is based on a constellation. Together, they split the year into 12 parts.

The zodiac signs are often shown in a wheel. They go in counterclockwise order.

Pisces is the 12th sign. Its time starts around February 19. It ends around March 20. People who are born during this time have Pisces as their **sun sign**.

FINAL SIGN

Astrology claims that being the last sign gives Pisces wisdom. The earlier signs are said to pass on lessons. Pisces takes them all in.

In northern parts of the world, Pisces's time comes near the end of winter.

Some people believe their sun signs can shape their futures. They also think signs affect how people think and act. For example, Pisces is linked to being kind and gentle.

FAST FACT

Pisces are known for forming deep friendships.

Pisces tend to think and feel deeply.

CHAPTER 3

ABOUT PISCES

The **glyph** for Pisces has three lines. The two outer lines stand for the fish. A center line is the rope. It links them together.

In pictures, the Pisces fish often swim opposite ways. They show the pull between real life and dreaming.

Pisces has water as its **element**. In astrology, water signs have strong ties to emotions. And Pisces are said to be very sensitive.

FAST FACT

Some people think Pisces can be **psychic**.

Like flowing water, Pisces can change to match what's around them.

Jupiter is the biggest planet in the solar system.

Astrology says ruling planets shape how people act. Pisces has two ruling planets. Long ago, Pisces was linked with Jupiter. Now, some people link it to Neptune instead.

TWO PLANETS

Jupiter is the planet of wisdom and growth. Neptune has ties to dreams and creativity. Pisces can fit with either planet. They can be open-minded and deep thinkers.

Neptune was the Roman god of the sea. And in astrology, water is linked with dreams and feelings.

CHAPTER 4

FEELING DEEPLY

Pisces are known for being imaginative, or good at making things up. Many create art. Famous Pisces include Rihanna, Millie Bobby Brown, and Olivia Rodrigo.

Olivia Rodrigo is a Pisces. She often shares her feelings through her songs.

Pisces are also known for being empathetic. They can sense how other people are feeling. And they care for others.

FAST FACT

Pisces often give great advice. They may work as **therapists**.

Pisces tend to be good at knowing how to help when friends are sad.

Spending time alone can help Pisces relax and recharge.

Pisces often put other people first. As a result, Pisces can get worn out. They may need to learn to take breaks and take care of themselves.

ESCAPING

Sometimes, other people's feelings can be too much for Pisces. When that happens, Pisces may try to escape. They may daydream. Or they may put off doing tasks. This can lead to problems.

COMPREHENSION QUESTIONS

Write your answers on a separate piece of paper.

1. Write a few sentences explaining the main ideas of Chapter 4.

2. Do you like to give other people advice? Why or why not?

3. Which ruling planet was Pisces linked with first?

   A. Jupiter
   B. Neptune
   C. Venus

4. How could having big imaginations help Pisces make art?

   A. Pisces could forget about their feelings.
   B. Pisces could do the same things that have worked before.
   C. Pisces could think of many new ideas.

5. What does **recorded** mean in this book?

*Pisces is one of the earliest **recorded** constellations. People first wrote about it thousands of years ago.*

A. written down
B. sounded out
C. taken apart

6. What does **empathetic** mean in this book?

*Pisces are also known for being **empathetic**. They can sense how other people are feeling. And they care for others.*

A. not paying attention to how others feel
B. knowing and caring how others feel
C. feeling angry often

Answer key on page 32.

GLOSSARY

constellation
A group of stars that form a shape.

element
One of four forces (air, earth, fire, or water) that each zodiac sign is matched with and said to be shaped by.

glyph
A shape that stands for a word or idea.

psychic
Able to see the future or read minds.

sensitive
Likely to have many feelings and share the feelings of others.

sun sign
A person's main zodiac sign, which is decided by the date they were born.

therapists
People trained to help others deal with feelings or challenges.

zodiac
The set of 12 signs used in astrology, based on a part of the sky that the sun appears to move through each year.

TO LEARN MORE

BOOKS

Betts, Bruce. *Neptune: Planet of Wind and Ice*. Lerner Publications, 2025.

Goldstein, Margaret J. *Mysteries of Stars*. Lerner Publications, 2021.

Loh-Hagan, Virginia. *Star Signs.* Cherry Lake Publishing, 2021.

ONLINE RESOURCES

Visit **www.apexeditions.com** to find links and resources related to this title.

ABOUT THE AUTHOR

Abby Doty is a writer, editor, and booklover from Minnesota. Her sun sign is Aquarius.

INDEX

ANSWER KEY:
1. Answers will vary; 2. Answers will vary; 3. A; 4. C; 5. A; 6. B